What to Expect When You're Expecting Larvae

Expecting Larvae

A GUIDE FOR INSECT PARENTS
(and Curious Kids)

Bridget Heos ILLUSTRATED BY **Stéphane Jorisch**

MILLBROOK PRESS · MINNEAPOLIS

For my three beloved larvae, Johnny, Richie, and J.J. —B.H.

To the little bugs who feast in my garden —S.J.

The author wishes to thank the following consultants for sharing their expertise:
Dr. Bruce Barrett, professor of entomology, University of Missouri (bees, butterflies, beetles, and doodlebugs)
Michele Brown, book conservator, Cornell University (books)
Dr. Deby Cassill, professor of biology, University of South Florida–Saint Petersburg (big-headed ants)
Dr. Mary Chamberlin, professor of biology, Ohio University (hornworms)
Helen Driscoll, rare bookseller (books)
Dr. Rhonda Hamm, entomologist, Cornell University (flies)
Dr. Frederick Stehr, entomologist, Michigan State University (bees, beetles, butterflies, moths, flies, and doodlebugs)
Dr. Gaye Williams, pest identification, Maryland Department of Agriculture (beetles)

Millbrook Press
A division of Lerner Publishing Group, Inc.
241 First Avenue North
Minneapolis, MN 55401 U.S.A.

Website address: www.lernerbooks.com

Library of Congress Cataloging-in-Publication Data

Heos, Bridget.
    What to expect when you're expecting larvae : a guide for insect parents (and curious kids) / by Bridget Heos ; illustrated by Stéphane Jorisch.
        p.   cm. — (Expecting animal babies)
    ISBN: 978-0-7613-5858-9 (lib. bdg. : alk. paper)
    1. Insects—Juvenile literature. 2. Insects—Infancy—Juvenile literature. 3. Insects—Larvae—Juvenile literature. I. Jorisch, Stéphane, ill. II. Title.
    QL467.2.H458 2011
    595.713'9—dc22   2010027294

Manufactured in the United States of America
1 – DP – 12/31/10

CONGRATULATIONS,
insect parent-to-be!

You must be so excited. You may be feeling proud but also a little scared. Your babies will be tiny. How will you help them grow big and strong, like you? Don't worry. You have instincts. They will tell you how to be a mother or a father.

If you're a daddy, your job is done. You fertilized the eggs. But mommies, you are still carrying the eggs. If you're curious about the bundles of joy inside, read on. Whether you are a butterfly or a bee, a moth or a fly, a beetle or even a bloodsucking mosquito, you'll find answers here to all your parenting questions.

chomp!

chomp!

Q. **What will my babies look like?**
Will they resemble their mother or father?

A. Surprise! Neither! They will look like worms. Whether your babies are wriggly maggots, fat grubs, or fuzzy caterpillars, your larvae will look different from you. Like many young insects, they are larvae. (One is a larva. Two are larvae.)

Wait a second. Are you a cicada, a cockroach, a dragonfly, a louse, or a praying mantis? If so, STOP reading. Your babies are nymphs, not larvae. Please see my companion guide: *Nymphs: They Look Like You . . . Only Even Smaller*. It's available at your local library. (Psst, cicadas, try not to make a lot of noise in there.)

Otherwise, carry on. But keep in mind that right now your babies are only teeny specks inside tiny eggs. Aren't you getting a little ahead of yourselves?

Q. That's right. Where should I lay my eggs?

A. Right smack dab in your larvae's favorite food. That's easy for you flies. You know what you're looking for. You may fly one or two miles past blushing roses, ripe tomatoes, and leafy trees. But those simply won't do. Then "Eureka!" you'll say. "I've found the dog doo of my dreams! (Or horse manure. Or trash heap. Or fill in the blank with your favorite muck.) My maggots will love it." And that's where you'll lay your eggs.

It's trickier if you're a butterfly. As a grown-up, you feed on the sweet liquid in flowers, called nectar. But your babies eat leaves. So you can't nibble on something to find out if it's yummy. Luckily, like many insects, you have taste buds on your feet. By standing on the leaves, you'll know if your youngsters will like them.

Q. How many babies will I have?

A. Usually, lots. If you're an oil beetle, prepare to welcome one thousand bouncing baby eggs. When they hatch, your larvae will crawl up flower stems and wait for a bee. They'll climb aboard and ride with it to its nest. There, your grubs will be bad houseguests. They'll gobble up the food meant for the bee larvae. They'll even eat the bee eggs! As a parent, you're probably embarrassed to hear this. But you did the same thing when you were young. Sadly, if a bee never arrives, your waiting larvae will not survive. You lay so many eggs in the hope that a few will make it to a bee's nest.

Some insects have smaller broods. If you're a dung beetle, you'll only have between two and five babies. You'll lay each egg inside a ball of dung, which is a polite way of saying poop. As larvae, your babies will eat their way out of the balls, growing into adults. Meanwhile, the dung will keep them safe and well fed. Your babies will all likely survive.

Whether you lay lots of eggs or only a few, it's the right number for you.

BURP

Chomp

Q. I fly. My wingless larvae can't come with me. What will they do all day?

A. They'll spend most of their time eating. Or more accurately, stuffing their faces! And it's no wonder. They are going through stages called instars, during each of which they can double their size. Imagine what this means:

1. As first instars, your larvae double their weight.

2. As second instars, they double their doubled weight.

3. As third instars, they double their doubled doubled weight.

4. As fourth instars . . . well, you get the idea.

And caterpillars sometimes grow even faster than that!

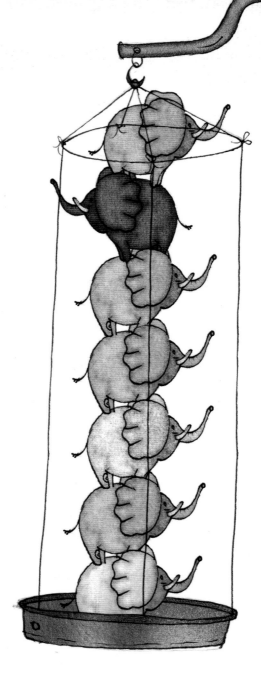

Depending on what kind of insect you are, your babies might go through these instars in a matter of days, weeks, or months. Rarely, it takes longer. Between instars, your larvae molt. That means they shed their skin (like a snake!), giving them room to grow.

If you are a sphinx moth, your hornworm caterpillar can eat a small tomato plant in one day. It can multiply its weight by ten thousand in just sixteen days. If a human baby grew this fast, the baby would soon weigh eighty thousand pounds—as much as seven elephants!

Q. Will my larvae eat what I eat?

A. Most likely you and your larvae will dine on different things.

Clothes moths, listen up. While you might not be hungry for wool now that you're grown-ups, your babies will be. Make sure they get proper nutrition. Check the sweaters and blankets where they sleep. Do they have holes? Good. Your babies are eating their fill.

If you're a mosquito, don't be alarmed if your larvae do not want to attack the arms and the legs of unsuspecting humans or bite a delicious squirrel or frog. Your offspring won't suck blood until they grow up. Even then, only your daughters will feast on blood. (Male mosquitoes never do. Instead, they dine on plant nectar.) While they're young, your offspring will live in ponds, lagoons, or puddles, where they'll munch on mouthwatering algae, bacteria, and fungi.

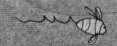

Are you a ladybug? Then you will need to share your food. You and your larvae (which look like tiny alligators) eat the same thing— bugs called aphids.

Now, now, don't be stingy. There are plenty of aphids for everybody. They give birth to fifty to one hundred nymphs at a time, and within eight days, their daughters have babies of their own.

(Aphids, please see *Nymphs: They Look Like You . . .
Only Even Smaller* for tips on avoiding these adorable yet
terrifying ladybugs.)

Q. Will anything eat my larvae?

A. Alas, yes. Dragonflies eat young mosquitoes. Some humans enjoy french-fried caterpillars, sautéed aquatic fly larvae, and bee larvae. And birds can't resist a plump, juicy grub worm. (Mmm . . . grub worms.) Woodpeckers are especially fond of these.

16

Note to wood-boring beetles: Woodpeckers are not only noisy but also evil. They drill holes in trees, searching for your larvae. Then they eat the poor little things!

Unfortunately, this is all part of the food chain. Your larvae eat trees. Woodpeckers eat your larvae. Cats, snakes, and hawks eat woodpeckers. Rest assured that many of your babies will manage not to be eaten. Instead, they'll live to enjoy meal after meal of delicious—and nutritious—wood.

Q. How will I keep my larvae safe?

A. You don't need to fret about that. It's a bug-eat-bug world, but nature has a few ways of protecting your babies.

One way is disguise—looking like something else. As a new caterpillar, the spicebush swallowtail looks like a bit of bird poop. When this larva sheds its skin and becomes bigger, it looks like a green snake. Scary!

Your larvae might blend in. This is called camouflage. If you're a wavy-lined emerald moth, your baby inchworm will stick flower petals to its back. That way, it looks like whatever flower it is eating.

thŕŕŕ...

Don't worry if your larvae don't have costumes and do stick out. This is another form of protection. When monarch butterfly caterpillars eat milkweed, they become poisonous. If a bird eats one, it gets sick. From then on, it's as if the caterpillar is saying, "Look at me! I have stripes. I'm yellow. I'm bright. Remember what happened last time you ate something striped, yellow, and bright? You threw up. You're not dumb enough to make that mistake again, are you?" And the bird leaves your caterpillar alone.

Finally, some insects have armies that offer protection. If you're a honeybee, you've got guards watching the entrance to your hive while young nurse bees (like teenage babysitters) feed your larvae "bee milk" and "bread" made of pollen and honey.

Q. I don't have a hive. Where will my babies sleep?

A. Most larvae rest wherever they eat—on leaves or underground, inside apples or bags of flour, in telephone poles, or even in this book!

However, beetle mothers should know that books aren't the ideal meals they once were. For one thing, glue tasted better in the old days. Books were bound with wheat, rice, or corn paste or with animal glue—made of bones, hoofs, and hides. Many types of beetle babies loved the old glues. They were nicknamed bookworms because they often curled up inside a good book.

NYMPHS:
They Look
Like You...
Only Even Smaller

Then somebody changed the glue recipe! Nowadays, book glue tastes like plastic. (Actually, it is plastic.) Also, libraries are not as inviting. They used to be damp, dusty, and dark—the perfect place to raise a family. Today's squeaky-clean bookshelves, on the other hand, are no place for larvae. Your babies would be better off inside a sack of peanuts or a nice box of chocolate.

Q. What will people think of my larvae?

A. Humans are funny about insects. They like some but not others.

If you are a butterfly, people will think your caterpillars are cute. They might even plant parsley or milkweed so that they can watch your babies grow.

But if you are a corn earworm moth, people probably won't like your hungry larvae. That's because they gobble up farmers' tomatoes, potatoes, and corn. This makes the farmers angry. They wanted to sell the vegetables or eat them.

And sorry, fly mommies and daddies. People think your maggots are yucky because they dine on trash, rotting food, dead animals, and poop. That is also what you eat. Or drink, rather. (Usually, larvae eat, but grown-up insects slurp the juice off things.)

Poor flies. I know what you're thinking. Shouldn't people like your maggots? They eat things humans don't want. Things like infections. Doctors put maggots on terrible wounds that won't heal. The maggots eat the dead tissue, making the person healthy again.

But not all maggots are cute little trash eaters. Some make people sick by living inside their bodies. We don't want to name any names, but . . . avoid the horrendous larvae of the screwworm fly.

Q. How fast will my babies grow up?

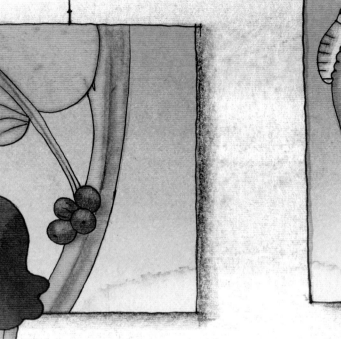

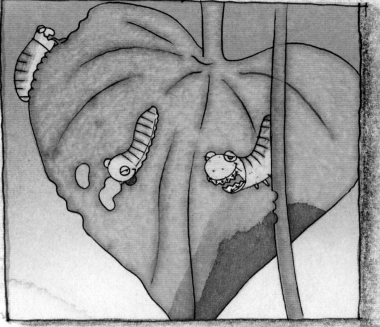

DiRection →

A. It could take days, weeks, or even years, depending on what kind of insect you are. Say your baby is a butterfly caterpillar. After eating and eating for a couple of weeks, one day, it stops. It grows still. Its skin shrivels. Don't worry. It's not sick.

Next, the skin behind its head splits open. Yikes! But this is only the chrysalis—or pupa—emerging. Inside the pupa, the larva re-creates itself. Days later, a butterfly breaks out, flaps its wings, and flies. For a human child, this would be like falling asleep and waking up as a giant bat! But for caterpillars, it is quite normal.

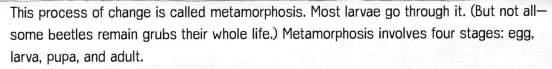

This process of change is called metamorphosis. Most larvae go through it. (But not all—some beetles remain grubs their whole life.) Metamorphosis involves four stages: egg, larva, pupa, and adult.

A butterfly pupa is a chrysalis. A moth pupa is a cocoon. Other insect pupas are just pupas, or pupae (pronounced PYU-pee), which is a funnier word.

Q. What should I do once my children have wings? Will I need to teach them how to fly?

A. I'm afraid there won't be time for that. By the time your young spread their wings, you will have passed away. Your children will know how to fly thanks to their instincts, just as you did at their age.

You've done your job. You left behind creatures just like you, even though they didn't start out looking that way.

Your young will grow up and mate and lay eggs that become new larvae, and the cycle starts all over again.

The new parents will ask, "What will my babies look like?"

Well, not really. But because it is a good question, we will ask it for them.

The End . . . and the Beginning.

GLOSSARY

algae: simple-celled organisms that live in water or damp places; to mosquito larvae, "Food!"

bacteria: simple-celled organisms that divide and multiply; to mosquito babies, "Dinner!"

bookworm: a beetle larva that is eating a book (the term refers to many different species); a person who reads too many books. Since you can never read too many books, let's change this to a person who reads many books.

broods: children in a family

caterpillar: the larva of a butterfly or a moth

chrysalis: the pupa of a butterfly

cocoon: the pupa of a moth. It has an extra layer of silk coating, as compared to a chrysalis.

egg: an oval or round object that may contain a developing insect, fish, bird, or reptile or, if you're lucky, candy

fertilized: began reproduction by causing sperm from the father to join with an egg from the mother

food chain: nature's way of making sure everybody gets enough to eat . . . until they get eaten themselves. Plants are eaten by animals. Those animals are eaten by other animals, which in turn are eaten by the next member in the chain.

fungi: plural of fungus; parasites that feed on living or dead things; another disgusting example of what mosquitoes eat; what humans sprinkle on their pizza and salad (Mushrooms are fungi.)

grub: the larva of a beetle; something people say before eating, as in: "Rub-a-dub-dub. Thanks for the grub." By *grub*, they mean "dinner," not baby beetles.

instars: the stages of a larva before and after it molts (sheds its skin)

instincts: built-in knowledge

larva: singular of larvae; the early stage of an animal, such as an insect, that goes through metamorphosis. Insect larvae look like short worms. But they're not worms. They're larvae.

maggot: a fly larva

metamorphosis: the changes insects go through as they develop from an egg to a larva to a pupa to an adult

nymphs: insect youngsters that look like their parents, only even smaller

pupa: singular of pupae, or pupas; for insects, that awkward stage between larva-hood and adulthood; the casing in which some insects transform from a larva into an adult

SELECTED BIBLIOGRAPHY

Butterfly Rainforest: Butterfly Q&A
http://www.flmnh.ufl.edu/butterflies/qanda.htm

Nuridsany, Claude, and Marie Perennou. *Microcosmos: The Invisible World of Insects*. New York: Stewart, Tabori & Chang, 1997.

Oldroyd, Harold. *The Natural History of Flies*. New York: W. W. Norton & Company, 1965.

O'Toole, Christopher, and Anthony Raw. *Bees of the World*. New York: Facts on File, 1991.

Schappert, Phil. *A World for Butterflies: Their Lives, Behavior and Future*. Buffalo: Firefly Books, 2000.

Stehr, Frederick, ed. *Immature Insects*. 2 vols. Dubuque, IA: Kendall Hunt Publishing Co., 1987.

FURTHER READING AND WEBSITES

BOOKS

Bishop, Nic. *Butterflies and Moths*. New York: Scholastic, 2009.
See photos of beautiful (and weird) butterflies and moths and learn more about their life cycles.

Posada, Mia. *Ladybugs: Red, Fiery, and Bright*. Minneapolis: Lerner Publications Company, 2002.
Rhyming text and bright illustrations show the life cycle and habits of ladybugs.

Swope, Sam. *Gotta Go! Gotta Go!* New York: Farrar, Straus and Giroux, 2004.
Come along with a cute monarch butterfly as it follows its instincts to Mexico.

Trueit, Trudi Strain. *Beetles*. New York: Benchmark Books, 2009.
Learn about the insect group that is 450,000 species strong and makes up 40 percent of all insects on Earth.

Walker, Sally M. *Mosquitoes*. Minneapolis: Lerner Publications Company, 2009.
Text and vivid photographs describe the physical characteristics, behavior, and habitat of these bloodsucking insects.

Zemlicka, Shannon. *From Egg to Butterfly*. Minneapolis: Lerner Publications Company, 2003.
Follow the life cycle of butterflies through simple text and colorful photographs.

WEBSITES

BugGuide
http://www.bugguide.net
At this site, naturalists share their knowledge of insects and identify bugs from photos taken all over the world.

The Children's Butterfly Site
http://www.kidsbutterfly.org
Sponsored by Montana State University, this website provides information and photographs of butterflies and moths as well as coloring sheets and teacher resources.

Pestworld for Kids
http://www.pestworldforkids.org
This site helps students write reports and create science projects about pests. It also provides teacher resources.

Science News for Kids
http://www.sciencenewsforkids.org
Read about science news in every discipline, learn about award-winning science fair projects, play games, and see how awesome science is. This website also includes teacher resources.

ABOUT THE AUTHOR

Bridget Heos is the author of twelve nonfiction books for older kids. This is her first picture book. She lives in Kansas City, Missouri, with her husband, three sons, and various larvae living in the yard—uninvited but welcome. She has thrown a birthday party for a caterpillar and once ate a scorpion.

ABOUT THE ILLUSTRATOR

Stéphane Jorisch is a full-time illustrator who has received several prestigious Canadian honors for his work, including a 1993 Governor General's Award, nominations for Governor General's Awards in 1995, 1997, and 1998, and nominations for the 1997 and 1999 Mr. Christie Book Awards. Jorisch works in a huge loft in Montreal, Quebec, with several other designers and illustrators. He believes that curiosity and a keen sense of observation are most important for an aspiring writer or artist.